ENORMOUS
BOOBS

ENORMOUS BOOBS

Summersdale Publishers Ltd
46 West Street
Chichester
West Sussex
PO19 1RP
UK

www.summersdale.com

Printed and bound in Great Britain

ISBN: 978-1-84953-181-8

Substantial discounts on bulk quantities of Summersdale books are available to corporations, professional associations and other organisations. For details contact Summersdale Publishers by telephone: +44 (0) 1243 771107, fax: +44 (0) 1243 786300 or email: nicky@summersdale.com.

ENORMOUS BOOBS

Stupidest Bloopers and Hilarious Headlines

RICHARD BENSON

summersdale

CONTENTS

INTRODUCTION

Boobs are funny. There is no getting away from the fact, and the truth is that the larger the boobs the more hilarious they are. So when we come across enormous boobs, it can be a real challenge to control ourselves.

Just be grateful that you are not the poor journalist who wrote the headline: 'Panda Mating Fails; Vet Takes Over' or the unfortunate jobseeker that included the following statement on their CV: 'I am great with the pubic'.

However, don't spend too much time feeling sorry for these unfortunate souls when you could be laughing at their blunders. After all, when push comes to shove, boobs may be funny, but enormous boobs are downright hilarious!

CLASSIFIED CLANGERS

Now is your chance to have your ears pierced and get an extra pair to take home, too.

FOR SALE:
2,000 pound wench

Tired of cleaning yourself?
Let me do it for you.

Handmade gifts for the
hard-to-find person.

Try our herbal remedies.
You can't get better.

WANTED:
man to take care of
cow that does not
smoke or drink.

For sale:
an antique desk suitable for lady
with thick legs and large drawers.

**RESERVE TICKETS FOR ANDREW
LLOYD WEBBER' SHIT MUSICAL.**

Ford grandad for sale.
£900ono

For sale.

Lovely rosewood piano. Owner going abroad with beautiful twisted legs.

North Wales Advertiser

FOR SALE:
Eight puppies from a German shepherd and an Alaskan hussy.

Used tombstone. Perfect for someone named Hendel Bergen Heinzel.

WASHING DONE – in my home including bachelors – Write Box 223 Call Chronicle.

Allentown Chronicle

PARKYNS – to the memory of Mr Parkyns, passed away September 10. Peace at last. From all the neighbours of Princes Avenue.

Leicester Mercury

If the motion were passed, no strike action would be taken by NALGO without a ballet of all its members.

Bristol Evening Post

Wrap poison bottles in sandpaper and fasten with scotch tape or a rubber band. If there are children in the house, lock them in a small metal box.

Philadelphia Record

Complete home for sale:
two double, one single bed, dining
room, three-piece suite, wireless,
television, carpets, lion, etc.

Portsmouth News

WOMAN WANTED to share fat with another.

CHILDREN SHOT FOR CHRISTMAS.

A photographer's advert in the

Morecambe Visitor

Time Out promoted a
'Master of Arts Degree in Deviancy'
at Middlesex Polytechnic.

Lesbian, 35, non smoker, loves horses, seeks same for friendship.

Personal ad in *Spare Rib*

Please save from destruction, three kitchens in desperate need of good homes.

Classified ad in *South Wales Evening Post*

City printers seek works manager, medium-sized but expanding.

Evening News

FAUX PAS AT THE PRESSES

Statistics show that teen pregnancy drops off considerably after age 25.

Army vehicle disappears after being painted with camouflage.

Scouts are saving aluminium cans, bottles, and other items to be recycled. Proceeds will be used to cripple children.

It turned out that it wasn't Mr Stone's regular doctor that treated him – just a young locust taking his place while he was on another call.

Remains found at the site are believed to be that of a Roman worrier.

A close colleague of the prime minister suggested he was beginning to show signs of metal fatigue.

A heavy pall of lust covered the upper two-thirds of Texas last night and was expected to drift south-east over the state by morning.

Yankton Press

Safety experts say school bus passengers should be belted.

When your flowers begin to fade,
stand in two inches of hot water.

Daily Sketch

Split and warmed and served with our cheese
you will be the envy of your guests.

From a catalogue for a New Hampshire store

The new lizard, 21 in. long, is said at the zoo
to be settling down well. It is described by
a keeper as being as lively as the cricketers
that are part of its favourite diet.

Lincolnshire Echo

A celebrated soprano was involved in a serious road accident last month. We are happy to report that she was able to appear this evening in four pieces.

Worthing Gazette

'The defendant is a married man with a young family; otherwise he is well behaved,' said a police representative.

New Zealand paper

Amazing luck in the Irish Sweep fell to a Kentish man who drew two tickets and a Sussex woman.

Yorkshire paper

Mr and Mrs Wyglass of New York have completed their holiday at Angus. They have been shooting tenants at Burgh House.

Dundee paper

Anyone can plant radishes; it takes courage to plant acorns and wait for the oats.

Boy Scouts Association Weekly

Impressed by the courtesy and friendliness of their Spanish-speaking guides, the Chileans reciprocated by inviting a number of air station officers to a farewell party aboard the *Esmeralda* on Tuesday evening. The *Esmeralda* sailed from San Francisco on Tuesday morning.

California paper

In Jonesboro, Arkansas, winds which reached eighty miles per hour caused minor property damage, and at Beebe, Arkansas, Mrs Sally Hill twisted her home from its foundations.

Oklahoma paper

The season for grass fires seems to have arrived, so stamp out that cigarette end before you throw it down.

Herne Bay Press

A reception immediately followed the ceremony with paper and flowers decorating the table, with the traditional tire wedding cake.

Nebraska paper

A cup of good English tea, with a few biscuits, is frequently his only food at breakfast, and this after he has devoured all the morning newspapers at nine o'clock.

Buckinghamshire paper

Congratulations to Mr Ralph L. Cobham on the girth of a son, who arrived on Wednesday.

Montevideo paper

It is a curious sight when the gardens are in bloom to watch dozens of artists squatting on their easels.

Australian paper

Mike McGrew, deputy US Marshall in Oklahoma City has carried his son's first baby as a good luck charm for thirteen years. He has had it hanging on the rear-view mirror of four automobiles and, during the war, kept it in the socks of his army uniform.

New Jersey paper

PEANUT-BUTTER GRILLED CORN –
Husk fresh corn; spread ears lightly with peanut butter. Wrap each ear with bacon slice; fasten with toothpick. Place on grill, turning until done – about 10 minutes. Or let everyone grill his own ears, using long skewers to do so.

The American Weekly

It is extremely difficult to tell the age of a snake unless you know exactly when it was born.

Detroit News

Anyone who breaks the law is at risk of being arrested.

Contra Costa Times

The ladies of the Merry Oldsters enjoyed a swap social on Friday evening. Everybody brought along something they no longer needed. Many ladies brought their husbands with them.

Pennsylvania Post

LAPSE IN CONSECRATION

THE ASSOCIATE MINISTER UNVEILED
THE CHURCH'S NEW TITHING
CAMPAIGN SLOGAN LAST SUNDAY:
I UPPED MY PLEDGE – UP YOURS.

**DON'T LET WORRY KILL YOU.
LET THE CHURCH HELP.**

For those of you who have children and don't know it, we have a nursery downstairs.

Tuesday at 4 p.m. there will be an ice cream social. All ladies giving milk will please come early.

The church is glad to have with us today as our guest minister the Rev. Green who has Mrs Green with him. After the service, we request that all remain in the sanctuary for the Hanging of the Greens.

Next Sunday, a special collection will be taken to defray the cost of the new carpet. All those wishing to do something on the new carpet will come forward and get a piece of paper.

The ladies of the church have cast off clothing of every kind and they may be seen in the church basement on Friday.

✝

Weight Watchers will meet at 7 p.m. at the first Presbyterian Church. Please use large double door at the side entrance.

MRS JOHNSON WILL BE ENTERING THE HOSPITAL THIS WEEK FOR TESTES.

Thursday at 5:00 p.m. there will be a meeting of the Little Mothers Club. All wishing to become little mothers will please meet the pastor in his study.

At the evening service tonight, the sermon topic will be 'What Is Hell?' Come early, and listen to our choir practice.

REMEMBER IN PRAYER THE MANY WHO ARE SICK OF OUR CHURCH AND COMMUNITY.

The service will close with 'Little Drops of Water.' One of the ladies will start quietly and the rest of the congregation will join in.

—————— † ——————

THIS BEING EASTER SUNDAY, WE WILL
ASK MRS BROWN TO COME FORWARD
AND LAY AN EGG ON THE ALTAR.

HAPLESS HEADLINES

MILK DRINKERS ARE TURNING TO POWDER

William Kelly was Fed Secretary

Hospitals are Sued by Seven Foot Doctors

**PANDA MATING FAILS;
VET TAKES OVER**

DRUG BARON HIDES CRACK IN PANTS

Council to Stamp on Dog Mess

Mayor Fights Erection in Town Square

*British Left Waffles
<u>on Falkland Islands</u>*

**SUN OR RAIN EXPECTED
TODAY, DARK LATER**

<u>Use Head to Avoid
Teen Pregnancy</u>

Weapons Found in Police Raid on Gun Shop

Water Shortages at Fire Scene – Firemen Forced to Improvise

WAR DIMS HOPE FOR PEACE

CONVICTS EVADE NOOSE AS JURY HUNG

Miners Refuse to Work After Death

Man Minus Ear Waives Hearing

THIEF GETS SIX MONTHS IN VIOLIN CASE

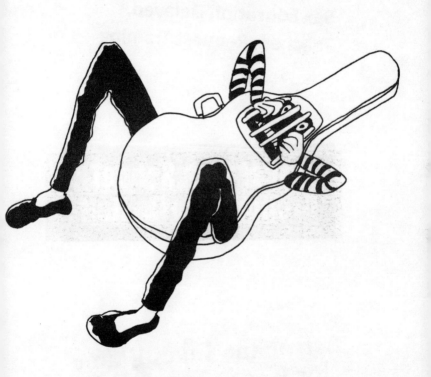

Sex Education Delayed,
Teachers Request Training

**Local High School
Dropouts Cut in Half**

Astronaut Takes Blame
for Gas in Spacecraft

KIDS MAKE NUTRITIOUS SNACKS

Red Tape Holds Up New Town Hall

Juvenile Court to Try Shooting Defendant

Prostitutes Appeal to Pope

Fireproof Clothing Factory
Burns to Ground

**FISH NEED WATER,
FEDS SAY**

**ONE-ARMED MAN APPLAUDS
THE KINDNESS OF STRANGERS**

Seven Judges Sit on Maid's Case

Yorkshire paper

STRIP CLUBS SHOCK — MAGISTRATES MAY ACT ON INDECENT SHOWS

Daily Mirror

USA WINS 1-1

Headline from the *New York Post* after the World Cup tie between England and the US

DON'T FOLLOW THE SIGNS

ARE YOU AN ADULT THAT
CANNOT READ?
If so, <u>we can help.</u>

<u>*OPEN*</u>
SEVEN DAYS A WEEK,
AND WEEKENDS TOO.

Why
go elsewhere
and pay too much?
<u>Come here first!</u>

Get 50 per cent off
OR
half price,
whichever is less.

BEWARE OF TRAINS GOING BOTH WAYS AT ONCE.

Notice at Durham level crossing

Let us quote a price to arrange your removal.

Sign in a Croydon furniture shop

**PERSONS ARE REQUESTED
NOT TO OCCUPY SEATS
WITHOUT CONSUMMATION.**

Notice in a Spanish cafe

*This play will be repeated tomorrow
night, so that those who missed it will
have the opportunity of doing so again.*

Sign outside a Dublin theatre

**Hot and cold baths under
personal supervision
of the proprietor.**

Notice in a Blackpool guest house

Free admission for old age
pensioners if accompanied
by both parents.

Sign outside a Scottish cinema

All water in this establishment has been passed by the manager.

Sign in a Dundee cafeteria

Leave your clothes here and go out and enjoy yourself.

Offer in an Edinburgh laundrette

Ladies are requested not to have children at the bar.

Sign in a Norwegian cocktail lounge

DIAGNOSIS: STUPID

- The patient refused an autopsy.

- The patient has no past history of suicide.

- She has had no rigors or shaking chills, but her husband states that she was very hot in bed last night.

'The surgeon said he'd removed my momentum — the funny apron of fat that covers the intestines.'

Healthy-appearing, decrepit 69-year-old white female, mentally alert, but forgetful.

The patient was in his usual state of good health until his aeroplane ran out of gas and crashed.

A transplant surgeon has called for a ban on 'kidneys-for-ale' operations.

Daily Mail

She is numb from her toes down.

By the time he was admitted, his rapid heart had stopped, and he was feeling better.

Patient gets chest pain if she lies on her left side for over a year.

· Exam of genitalia reveals
that he is circus sized.

The patient's past medical history
has been remarkably insignificant
with only a 40 pound weight
gain in the past three days.

She slipped on the ice and
apparently her legs went in
separate directions in early December.

The patient left the hospital feeling much better except for her original complaints.

 Nonverbal, uncommunicative and offers no complaints.

Discharge instructions:

· drink plenty of urine.

ORDER:

· please feed patient only when awake.

The Worksop Bugle carried a news report about a man who'd 'recovered from a tuna of the kidney'.

The first essential in the treatment of burns is that the patient should be removed from the fire.

First Aid Manual

SPORTING
SLIP-UPS

Graeme Souness went behind my back right in front of my face.

Craig Bellamy

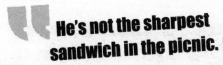

He's not the sharpest sandwich in the picnic.

Tony Cascarino

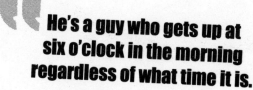

He's a guy who gets up at six o'clock in the morning regardless of what time it is.

Colin Cooper on Paul Tito,
New Zealand rugby player

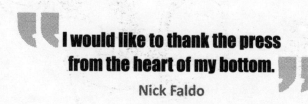

I would like to thank the press
from the heart of my bottom.

Nick Faldo

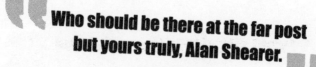

Who should be there at the far post but yours truly, Alan Shearer.

Colin Hendry

One of the reasons Arnie (Arnold Palmer) is playing so well is that, before each tee-shot, his wife takes out his balls and kisses them – oh my God, what have I just said?

US TV commentator

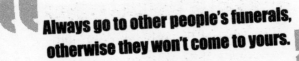

Always go to other people's funerals, otherwise they won't come to yours.

Yogi Berra

I want all the kids to copulate me.

Andre Dawson

Everybody line up alphabetically according to their height.

Casey Stengel

So, Woosie, you're from Wales. What part of Scotland is that?

American journalist to Ian Woosnam during a 1987 press conference

> **An inch or two either side of the post and that would have been a goal.**
>
> Dave Bassett

> **He's got his hands on his knees and holds his head in despair.**
>
> Peter Jones

> **He had an eternity to play that ball... but he took too long over it.**
>
> Martin Tyler

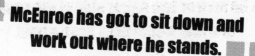

McEnroe has got to sit down and work out where he stands.

Fred Perry

These ball boys are marvellous. You don't even notice them. There's a left handed one over there. I noticed him earlier.

Max Robertson

This is really a lovely horse and I speak from personal experience since I once mounted her mother.

Ted Walsh

> ## The racecourse is as level as a billiard ball.

John Francombe

> **I owe a lot to my parents, especially my mother and father.**

Tana Umaga

> **The lead car is absolutely, truly unique, except for the one behind it which is exactly identical to the one in front of the similar one in back.**

Grand Prix race announcer

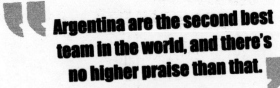

> **Argentina are the second best team in the world, and there's no higher praise than that.**

Kevin Keegan

> **The most vulnerable area for goalies is between their legs.**
>
> Andy Gray

> **Andy Ellis – the 21-year-old who turned 22 a few weeks ago...**
>
> Murray Mexted

LOST IN
TRANSLATION

A chicken company's slogan, 'It takes a tough man to make a tender chicken', was translated into Spanish as, 'It takes a sexually stimulated man to make a chicken affectionate'. Billboards throughout Mexico were emblazoned with the slogan along with a picture of the company's owner next to a chicken.

The car manufacturer Ford had difficulty releasing its Pinto in Brazil because *pinto* in Portuguese is slang for 'small male genitalia'. Similarly, the Vauxhall Nova struggled to sell in Spanish-speaking countries because in Spanish '*No va*' means 'It does not go'.

When Pepsi first started exporting to Taiwan they decided to use the slogan 'Come Alive with the Pepsi Generation'. This was translated into Chinese far too literally as 'Pepsi brings your ancestors back from the grave'.

When advertising their new ballpoint pen in Mexico, Parker chose the slogan 'It won't leak or embarrass you' to front the campaign. Unfortunately they made the mistake of thinking the Spanish word for embarrass was *embarazar* so their slogan ended up reading 'It won't leak in your pocket and make you pregnant'.

INCOMING
Salad of the time
Selection of Catalan Sausages – quarter note and white
Soup of having cooked
Rape – the fisherman style
Greenness (according to the season)

MEATS
You throw veal to the coal
Chicken to the ember
Catalan sausage with Jewish (Dry)

PROSTRATE
Ice creams 'he/she requests letter'
Honey and I kill
Tart of the house

COVERS AND APPETIZERS
Veal balls
Small bombs

TOASTED BREAD
'All I smelled'
To the pleasure or half and half

Menu in Richard Guise's travelogue

Two Wheels Over Catalonia

Umbro decided to use the German word for 'cyclone' as a name for some of their footwear. Unfortunately, the German word *zyklon* is also the name of the gas that was used in Nazi concentration camps.

The Dairy Association's slogan 'Got Milk?' was translated into Spanish as 'Are you lactating?'

Scandinavian vacuum manufacturer Electrolux used the following in an American campaign: 'Nothing sucks like an Electrolux'.

American Airlines wanted to make customers in Mexico aware of the new leather first class seats available on their planes. They translated their 'Fly in leather' slogan very literally and Spanish readers found themselves asked to 'Fly naked'.

KFC's famous 'finger-lickin' good' strapline went terribly wrong in the Chinese market. It was literally translated as 'eat your fingers off'.

Coors' slogan 'Turn it loose' was translated into Spanish as 'Suffer from diarrhoea'.

An American clothing manufacturer printed T-shirts for the Spanish market which promoted a visit by the Pope. Instead of their shirts saying 'I Saw the Pope' in Spanish, they actually said 'I Saw the Potato'.

Kellogg's, the famous cereal producer, wanted to introduce a new cereal brand called 'Bran Buds' in Sweden. However, after translation, it was written as 'burned farmer'.

An American cooking oil brand did not do very well with their sales in South America because the brand name was translated into Spanish as 'Jackass Oil'.

When the James Bond film *Dr No* was released in Japan the title was translated as *No Need for a Doctor*.

BOOB JOBS

I worked for six years as an uninformed security guard.

My hobbies include raising long-eared rabbis as pets.

I am great with the pubic.

- **Seeking a party-time position with potential for advancement.**

Work Experience:
Dealing with customers' conflicts that arouse.

Objective:
- to have my skills and ethics challenged on a daily basis.

Personal goal:
To hand-build a classic cottage from
the ground up using my father-in-law.

I am about to enrol on a Business and
Finance Degree with the Open University.
I feel that this qualification will prove
detrimental to me for future success.

Hobbies:
* *enjoy cooking Chinese and Italians.*

- **Consistently tanked as top sales producer for new accounts.**

Planned new corporate facility at $3 million over budget.

Revolved customer problems and inquiries.

I'm a rabid typist.

**Marital Status:**
**Unmarried bachelor.**

. . . .

**Served as assistant
sore manager.**

Objection:
• to utilise my skills in sales.

Objectives: ten-year goal:
- total obliteration of sales and federal income taxes and tax laws.

Excellent memory, strong maths aptitude, excellent memory, effective management skills and very good at maths.

CORRECT ME IF I'M WRONG...

In a recipe for salsa published recently, one of the ingredients was misstated, due to an error. The correct ingredient is '2 tsp. of cilantro' instead of '2 tsp. of cement'.

Due to incorrect information received from the Clerk of Courts Office, Diane K. Merchant, 38, Mrs, was incorrectly listed as being fined for prostitution in Wednesday's paper. The charge should have been failure to stop at a railroad crossing. *The Public Opinion* apologises for the error.

A Nov. 26 article in the District edition of *Local Living* incorrectly said a Public Enemy song declared 9/11 a joke. The song refers to 911, the emergency phone number.

A story that appeared in Sunday's *Argus Observer* contained an incorrect spelling of a name. Pastor Dick Bigelow was incorrectly identified as Dick Bigblow. *The Argus Observer* regrets the error.

Some confusion arose in a review of a television drama about knife crime as a result of mishearing the term shanking, which means stabbing someone with a knife, as shagging.

The Guardian

Our story on the price of tomatoes last week misquoted Alistair Petrie, general manager of Turners and Growers. Discussing the price of tomatoes, Petrie was talking about retail rate not retail rape. We apologise for the misunderstanding.

Sunday Star-Times, New Zealand

In an article of 6 November 2007 about Tom Sykes, a freelance journalist, we mistakenly included a photograph of Tom Sykes a digital TV consultant and his family. We wish to make it clear that the latter is not a recovering alcoholic or drug addict, and apologise for the error.

Daily Mail

Australian cricketer Don Bradman was carried, not curried, off the field during the Ashes series in August 1938 (Heroic Hutton leads England to 903, page 12, the archive, November 6).

The Guardian

We misspelled the word misspelled twice, as mispelled, in the Corrections and Clarifications column on September 26, page 30.

The Guardian

David Marr unfortunately misquoted me in 'A fallen leader of faith' (August 4-5). I actually said that I endured the naked beatings, paternal bum caresses, etc. from Frank Houston, not enjoyed them. I can assure readers that the experience wasn't pleasurable but painful, both at the time and for some years later.

Peter Laughton Carrara (Qld)

Sydney Morning Herald

A Nov. 19 article about a new study indicating that Detroit is the most dangerous US city incorrectly stated that Detroit has seen nearly one million people killed since 1950. In fact, that number represents the overall decline in Detroit's population since 1950, not the number of people killed. *The Star* regrets the error.

Toronto Star

Big Brother's Carole is a sexual health worker, not a sex worker, which usually means something rather different.

The Mirror

We wrongly converted a baby's birth weight of 8 lbs 15 oz as 51 kg. It is 4.1 kg. A 51 kg baby is an impossible 112 lbs 6 oz.

The Guardian

DID I REALLY SAY THAT?

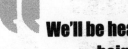

> **They seem cold out there, they're rubbing each other and he's only come in his shorts.**

Michael Buerk on watching Philippa Forrester cuddle up to a male astronomer for warmth during BBC1's UK eclipse coverage

> **We'll be heading for the deepening heights of recession.**

Economic spokesperson

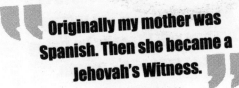

> **Originally my mother was Spanish. Then she became a Jehovah's Witness.**

Geri Halliwell

> **The Miss World competition is still popular even if it has its fair share of knockers.**

Julia Morley

> **I've got taste. It's inbred in me.**

David Hasselhoff

> **Anyone buying this record can be assured that the money they pay will literally be going into someone's mouth.**

Bob Geldof

> **We would have no coal industry if the miners are driven into the ground.**

Claire Brooks

> **I believe you're a fourth generation chef. What did your father do?**

Lucy Freud

> **We're going to move left and right at the same time.**

Jerry Brown

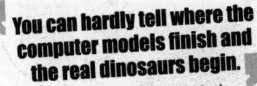

" You can hardly tell where the
computer models finish and
the real dinosaurs begin. "

Laura Dern on *Jurassic Park*

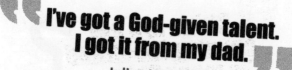

I've got a God-given talent.
I got it from my dad.

Julian Wakefield

We all know that a leopard
cannot change his stripes.

Al Gore

Let this be a silent
protest that will be heard
throughout the country.

Tim Leddin

That's the way the
cookie bounces.

Vic Schiro

China is a big country, inhabited by many Chinese.

Charles de Gaulle

Those who survived the San Francisco earthquake said, 'Thank God, I'm still alive.' But, of course, those who died, their lives will never be the same again.

Barbara Boxer, US Senator

And now, will y'all stand and be recognised.

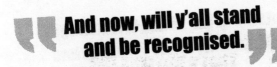

Gib Lewis, Texas Speaker of the House to a group of people in wheelchairs on Disability Day

> **This is Preservation Month. I appreciate preservation. It's what you do when you run for president. You gotta preserve.**
>
> George W. Bush

> **I was recently on a tour of Latin America, and the only regret I have was that I didn't study Latin harder in school so I could converse with those people.**
>
> Dan Quayle

> **Outside of the killings, Washington DC has one of the lowest crime rates in the country.**
>
> Mayor Marion Barry

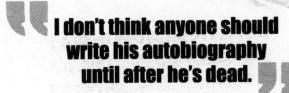

I don't think anyone should
write his autobiography
until after he's dead.

Samuel Goldwyn

That's a self-portrait
of himself by himself.

Richard Madeley

I think that gay marriage should
be between a man and a woman.

Arnold Schwarzenegger

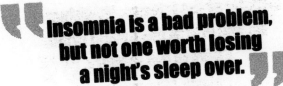

Insomnia is a bad problem,
but not one worth losing
a night's sleep over.

Goronwy Jones